Marathon of Heroes
A Lands of Lunacy adventure for 4–6 level 5 characters from **Fail Squad Games.**

Writing
Ric Martens & Lloyd Metcalf

Artwork
Lloyd Metcalf, Raven Metcalf, Rick Hershey of Fat Goblin Games, Jeremy Hartillos

Editor in Chief
G. Scott Swift

This adventure is intended to be used with the **Lands of Lunacy** setting guide. The setting guide is NOT required to play through the Marathon of Heroes; the GM may simply ignore references specific to the setting. The Lands of Lunacy setting is available primarily from **FailSquadGames.com.** You may also find it on Amazon, Barnes & Noble, and many other fine RPG retailers.

How to use this module
Flavor text is shaded and boxed, intended to be read aloud to players to aid you (the GM) in describing the setting and scenes. Monster details are listed in the Appendix. Statistics for some standard monsters can be found in your favorite Manual of Monsters (page numbers indicated where appropriate). Abbreviations for game books commonly associated with the fifth edition of the world's favorite fantasy roleplaying game are as follows. PHB, DMG, and MM reference the player's guide, game master guide, and manual of monsters respectively.

Marathon of Heroes Afflictions
Lands of Lunacy (Marathon of Heroes) affliction tables are provided as a suggested replacement for the general setting affliction tables in the setting guide.
Magic control is variable throughout the adventure (depending on the current domain). Refer to the Magic section at the beginning of each trial for details.

Players
If you are a reading this and you are a player, STOP READING NOW and give this adventure module to your Game Master or referee. Reading through the adventure as a player compromises the enjoyment of the adventure for all involved.

RPG Crate
This adventure's first release was made possible by the generous gamers subscribed to RPG Crate and supporters of Fail Squad Games.

Theme
The theme of this adventure is the marathon. There are four sections broken down into 6.5 mile runs (26 miles), but it's the last short section that is utter (and literal) hell.

The Marathon of Heroes is broken down into four sections to challenge the core classes of the game: fighter, magic-user, cleric, and thief. Each of these classes, and those derived from them, have an opportunity to shine in their own sections. Characters out of their element attempting to proceed through those sections should find it challenging or nearly impossible. This adventure champions the balanced party approach and strategy of class diversity. By the time the heroes reach the fifth and final segment of the adventure, they should find themselves a unified, well-oiled machine.

Regarding Lands of Lunacy

The Lands of Lunacy, in brief, are made up of various pocket dimensions surrounded by the Chaos Void. These pocket dimensions are referred to as domains. Domains are typically ruled by and exist to support a lordly entity or ruling power. The Chaos Void is an ever-shifting plane of ultimate chaos and nothingness.

Each domain has its own varying rules of physics and effects on non-native visitors. Entry and exit from these domains is done so through portals or powerful magics that are dictated by the phases of moons or the utter chaos of the void in which the dimensions are immersed. Non-natives to the Lands of Lunacy are frequently referred to as **banals** and are affected in various ways by the Chaos Void and the Lands of Lunacy.

Sanity Points in the Lands of Lunacy

Sanity is tracked much like hit points. As such, each banal has a pool of Sanity points, and various events, creatures, and situations can drain them away and will eventually weaken the victim's grasp on reality.

Some creatures within the Lands of Lunacy attack sanity directly, feeding off organized thought. Other times, sanity can slip away as the veil between the domain and the Chaos Void breaks down. Sometimes all it takes is the stress of adventure or the knowledge of what lies beyond the barrier of the domain to sap the willpower of the banal mind.

Keeping one's sanity is primarily a battle of willpower. Sanity points are calculated by adding the Wisdom score and 3 points per character level of experience. For example, a fifth level character with a Wisdom of 12 would have 27 Sanity points (12+15).

It is up to the GM or the adventure module in use to determine when Sanity points are at a risk for loss and

whether a saving throw to prevent the loss applies. Many Lands of Lunacy adventures have built-in mechanics for Sanity point loss, but the GM is encouraged to adjudicate Sanity point loss for characters exploring these unhinging worlds whenever appropriate.

Sanity points may be restored with quiet rest, removed from stress or trauma. Sanity points restore themselves at 1d4 plus Wisdom modifier per long rest [8hrs] unless they reach 2 or less *(see Levels of Madness section in the Lands of Lunacy setting guide)*. Clerical curative spells for physical wounds do not cure sanity. Clerics of the domains, however, may have mental healing spells that do heal sanity in similar ways.

If you do not have access to the Lands of Lunacy setting guide, the following is a general guide:

- Sanity 2 to 0: Temporary Insanity

- Sanity -1 to -8: Intermediate Lingering Insanity (Recover 1 point every 2 days)

- Sanity -9 to -16: Permanent Insanity (Permanent mental damage)

- Sanity -17 or less: Lost to Madness (No recovery)

Mists of Lunacy

Throughout this adventure the player characters will be exposed to banks of mist, some avoidable, some not. The mist banks, known as Mists of Lunacy, are areas where the Chaos Void comes in contact with the Prime Material Plane. The merging of the two planes creates an odd energy that affects mental stability. The sanity of the PCs will be tested again and again.

When exposed to the mists, player characters must make an INT save [DC 15] or suffer 1d4 points of Sanity damage. Those so affected have an additional 50% chance of suffering effects from the afflictions table in the corresponding adventure area.

Adventure Overview

The heroes are gathered by Lord Gelton Fez as the most renowned freelance adventurers in the area. In his hold, he retains the heroes to address a red dragon problem that is fast encroaching on his land and people. He has discovered that a volcanic island out to sea is the home of the creature. Lord Fez has lost many heroes and men pursuing the beast and seeking its lair and is now left with the brave heroes (at the table) to resolve his woes and save his people.

Lord Fez introduces the heroes to their captain and first mate and implores them to set sail to the isle with all haste.

Along the way, the crew is inflicted with a sudden madness, and most are lost to the seas, among them, the first mate, or so it is assumed.

Upon landing on the isle, the heroes are met by a friendly murine (an anthropomorphic rodent) who warns them that they are not prepared to meet the fiery hatred of the dragon. They also may discover that they are no longer on the island they intended. They have been transported to the Lands of Lunacy.

Four 6.5 mile tests and challenges follow, each based on one of the four prime character classes of fantasy role playing games: fighter, magic-user, cleric, and thief. In their turn, each is in the spotlight supported by the rest of the party.

The heroes, with the guidance of their murine friend, must conquer each leg of the marathon: Fighter's, Magic-user's, Cleric's, and Thief's Challenges (totaling 26 miles of quests).

At last they have prepared, been rewarded, and find themselves ready to face the dragon! This is a brutal fight, but the party may gain a few allies that help them achieve victory.

The last section of the marathon is through hell on earth as they race to battle their dragon foe.

After returning to the ship eager to set sail away from the isle with the heroes' proof of the slain dragon, they find the captain slain by beasts and the first mate washed up on shore.

During the return journey, laden with treasure, the scoundrel of a first mate reveals himself as an assassin. He attempts to kill the heroes and return victorious with the treasure AND the praise of Lord Fez. The heroes may not see their home shores again if they let their guard down.

Upon returning to the shores with proof of their kill, the townsfolk rejoice, and the lord calls an audience. The heroes are victorious and return more powerful than ever.

Can the heroes survive this deadly foray into the mysterious realm of chaos? Only the players' wits and a few lucky die rolls stand between victory and defeat.

A Call to Heroes

You are all gathered at the table in the war room of Lord Gelton Fez's keep. You were each requested to appear as you are the most renowned freelance heroes of the lands over which Lord Fez rules.

The messengers were rather vague about the request and the purpose of the call for your presence, but after some introductions and some basic conversation, one theme is consistent—danger and great amounts of wealth lie before you.

Give the players a moment to describe their characters and introduce themselves if they are new to the gaming table or party. If your group is already acquainted, assume the call was for the heroes as a collective.

The main door to the war room swings open as a young, handsome, dark-skinned man confidently strides to the table.

"Greetings heroes. Thank you for heeding my call in our time of need. I won't mince words. I have a dangerous request to make of you, and the rewards for risking your lives may be beyond your wildest fantasies.

"Heroes , we have a dragon problem! And not just any dragon problem, the greediest of all dragon-kind, a great red! The evil beasts are certainly known for their wickedness and are absolutely legendary in their hoarding of riches and magic.

"The creature has been razing farms and homes of outlying villages, but its eventual path is leading directly toward the city and the heart of this kingdom! We are not equipped to defend against a dragon assault.

"I cannot fault any of you for being afraid to pursue this challenge I lay before you. You may freely leave with my thanks and no ill will from myself or my keep.

"Should you stay, I ask only that you return with the head of the dragon and 40% of the creature's hoard to fill my people's empty coffers.

"At great cost of both lives and gold, we have tracked the beast to an isle two days off the coast. I will supply you with a ship and crew to take you there. Our townsfolk will equip you with armor and weapons as best they can for the trials ahead.

"What say you my heroes of legend? Hunters of the Red Menace? Champion of the people? Do you answer this call in our time of need? Do you wish to return with such riches that make kings blush?"

Lord Fez supplies the heroes with any non-magical weapons, armor, and basic equipment that they require. He cannot provide a large amount of funds prior to the journey as hunting the dragon and rebuilding the outlying lands has truly drained the coffers.

If the Heroes Accept

"There is hope for this domain after all! I am heartened and grateful that you have stayed to defend our people in these dark times!

"I have retained the finest captain the seas have ever known and her vessel to take you to the dragon's isle.

"May I introduce Sasha von Bairn and her first mate James Millerson. Sasha has served on our fleets for some time and has proven herself both hearty, clever, and capable on the sea.

"Her first mate, James, can read the seas like no other. If there is a more capable ship and crew on the oceans of this world, they are only known to Davy Jones Locker.

Sasha wastes no time with polite banter.
"My ship is the Sea Sylph. She's lucky, strong, and fast. On my ship, it's *MY* command. If we are clear on that, I can get you to your island and home in one piece, that is, if you survive what awaits you ashore."

Sasha von Bairn is a solid warrior and a very capable leader. She is a weathered, but powerful 32-year-old sailor that leaves no room for high society politics. Her crew of eight regulars respect her and are loyal to the end. They are possibly the envy of all ships in the fleet. The crew of the Sea Sylph are well fed, have a say in operations, and rarely leave port without a supply of rum. Expectations of the crew on the Sea Sylph are high, but so are the rewards.

James is quiet and stern. His focus is to carry out the captain's orders in excruciating detail. He makes no social banter at all and sees no reason to share friendship with passengers he is sure are headed to their flaming deaths. He notes every item the heroes bring aboard the Sylph in his personal log when they board. He notes every dagger, ration, flask, and bit of string. He claims it is to account for cargo weight and the speed of the Sylph. If challenged, Captain Bairn enforces the request to detail the inventory. She is confident in James' request, and he has always kept detailed records of the ship's cargo. The crew have come to see his accounting as a lucky ritual before setting sail.

The crew of the Sylph, for statistical purposes, consists of 6 bandits, a bandit leader, and a commoner (an orphaned cabin boy named Jacob). The bandit leader is Wilhelm Vestin, who acts as a lieutenant of marines or commander of the crew for basic orders.

The Sea Sylph

The Sea Sylph is a triple lateen rigged caravel ship with modifications made by Sasha and the crew. They have managed to arrange cargo holds and sails in such a way as to maximize the usefulness and speed of the vessel. Prior to setting sail, James adjusts ballast stones in the hull to exacting precision. Even loaded with cargo, the Sylph rides high in the water and remains agile.

Sasha keeps the regular crew to a minimum to maximize speed, minimize reward division, and maximize loyalty.

The average speed of the Sylph is 6 knots (roughly 7 MPH) in average wind on open water. The island of the dragon is roughly 200 miles off the coast. The journey requires 2 full days, taking variables of wind and tacking into account.

On the Sea

Deep in the night, the watch blows the horn of attack. The crewmembers throw open the hatch and scramble to grab weapons, clubs, and torches.

Above deck, a watchman has a tentacle wrapped around his leg and is being pulled over the rail by a wicked looking creature that can only be described as half man/half octopus.

Numerous tentacles can be seen at the rails as ten of the gruesome creatures pull themselves aboard.

Out at sea, the Sylph begins to shine. She clips along all day with a steady side-wind. Well into the second watch of the night, the deck is boarded by 10 cephalugia who attempt to drag the occupants into the sea. In the water, they have called on the aid of giant electric eels to stun their victims as they hit the water.

The Foggy Approach

On the evening of the second day, the fiery isle of the dragon glows on the horizon, and the sea feels calm. A heavy fog bank has rolled in, blocking all but the soft glow of the volcano from sight.

"AHHH the Sylph is ablaze!!" cries one of the hands.

"Abandon ship, she's burning up!" Wailing in terror and agony, the deckhand jumps overboard.

No flames are visible anywhere aboard the Sylph.

The wall between the Prime Material Plane and the Chaos Void is thin here. Because of the thin fabric between the two planes, a passage into the Lands of Lunacy exists here. Vatrastrom knows about this passage and feels it adds another level of secrecy and security to his lair.

When she entered the mists, the Sylph and all aboard passed into the Lands of Lunacy. The delusional deckhand is the first to experience madness. Other deckhands continue to lose their grip on sanity, and all hands must make an INT save [DC 15] or suffer the effects of madness (table below). Player characters must also make an INT save DC 15 or suffer 1d4 points of Sanity damage. Those so affected have an additional 50% chance of suffering the effects on the table below.

Sanity Effects of the Mists (at sea)	
1	Fear (1d4) – 1. Frozen with terror, 2. Attack any creature within 5', 3. Leap overboard to flee, 4. Permanent insanity from terror.
2	Victims believe they are a cephalugia and wish to return to the sea (attempt to drag others under with them).
3	Convinced the entire crew has turned evil, the victim fights anyone within 10' to the death.
4	Hallucinations – visions range from euphoric beauty to gruesome nightmares.
5	Skin crawlers – Victims are convinced that there are burrowing insects beneath their skin and begin digging out the imaginary creatures. (Damage depends on means used to dislodge the crawlers.)
6	Neptune's call – Victims hear the call of the sea god and desire to join him at the bottom of the sea.

When the mists roll in, Sasha and James automatically make their saving throws and are not affected by the lunacy. During the plague of lunacy, the first mate, James Millerson, goes missing. Sasha easily assumes he is lost to the sea. However, he has used a Scroll of Invisibility and hidden in the hull with the ballast stones.

His plan is to wait out the heroes. Either Sasha and the crew are slain and he claims the Sylph, or the heroes return successfully with plenty of treasure. If it's the latter, a simple "accident" at sea is all it takes for him to return as a hero of the people and richer than a king.

Any characters flying or levitating above the mists to orient themselves, see only a dark, heavily forested island dead ahead.

Shortly after being caught in the mists, the Sylph nearly runs aground on the sandy shore.

A Friend in Chaos

From the mists, a dark forested island comes into view directly ahead of the Sylph.

Sasha presses the ship hard to port and kicks free the anchor for an abrupt and jarring halt. She immediately barks orders to drop all sails.

Even with the quick action the ship nearly runs ashore and will need to be oared back before low tide.

"Closer than I thought heroes," Sasha says, "According to the charts, we are 26 miles from the isle yet. Without James I am less confident, but I have guided ships long enough. The last glimpse I had of the stars, I honestly didn't recognize half of them. Something here isn't right."

If the party attempts to sail on around the isle, they find themselves facing another isle (in fact, the same island) in a similar fashion. The mists and stars redirect the ship, creating disorientation to return to the isle. Constant sailing through the sea results in more cephalugia and eel attacks or something worse.

The party has entered a Lands of Lunacy pocket dimension—the center of which is the island that follows.

Once ashore, the heroes are met by a murine named Gundastav. He approaches cautiously with his hands outstretched in a non-threatening posture.

The murine, a humanoid rodent race native to the Lands of Lunacy domains, are generally kind and helpful.

"Friends, my name is Gundastav. I'm so glad I have found you. You have come to challenge the dragon, haven't you?

"You will not win, not now, not this way. His isle is part of the Lands of Lunacy and exists in a domain that phases in and out of your own world.

"You may reach the isle, but you will surely perish. My people have lived under his reign of terror for some time, and I've been sent to help you, if you'll accept it.

"Though the murine have never been powerful enough to defeat the dragon, we are not without resources. My ancestors foretold that a mighty group of heroes would come to our land one day to liberate us. To both test and reward the heroes, my ancestors created a number of challenges we call the Marathon of Heroes.

"If you complete the Marathon of Heroes, you will have the weapons and tools to defeat **Vatrastrom**. Yes, that's his name, and now that you know it, you have some power over him.

"You are in the Lands of Lunacy, and these domains lead the way to a secret entrance to Vatrastrom's lair and the tools to defeat him.

"You can save the murine, yourselves, and many others. You may return to your ship now to charge the creature's lair or you may flee, but you may also proceed to the Marathon of Heroes. It's 26 miles to the entrance of the lair of the wicked wyrm where you may yet abscond with his treasures and save us all.

"Sit, share my mead if you like, and decide your fate. But decide quickly, for his eye will be on you soon. Choose a stone from the beach to begin the Marathon of Heroes.

"It seems the lands have offered you opportunities that very few ever see."

The Stones

Five large, smooth, round stones with sigils burnt into them are set into the sand on the beach: one with a sword, one with a star, one with ball of fire, one with a key, and a final stone in the center of the others with the profile of a dragon.

All stones pulse softly with a bluish light and will cease pulsing when the challenge is finished. The challenges need not be completed in any order, or even attempted at all. Touching the dragon sigil will teleport the PCs to the dragon isle where they must escape through the lava tubes and out the dragon's lair.

The Sylph is waiting on the beach of the isle of the dragon's lair.

If any one of the party touches a stone for more than 5 seconds, it is accepted as the "chosen path" and will teleport the entire party.

The Fighter's Challenge

The Domain

This challenge ends at the center of the island. It is 6.5 miles from the outside beach to the island center. Flying, by spells or the natural flying ability of creatures, functions only briefly. Non-natives attempting to fly may do so for no more than 2 rounds before they find themselves lost in the forest at a random location in a state of exhaustion. This is the effect of grazing the barrier between the edge of the domain and the Chaos Void. Levitation spells function more reliably, but start to fall apart 50 feet above the treetops.

In the Fighter's Challenge, magic is weak and all spells cast have a 20% chance of complete failure. Targets have +1 to all saves, and damage dice from spells suffer a -1 penalty. Healing spells also suffer a -1 per hit die penalty on healing effects.

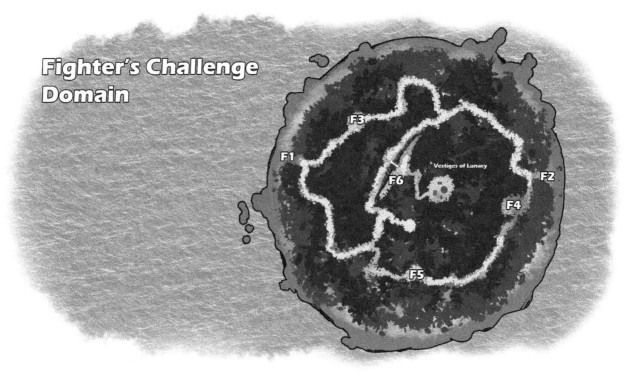

Fighter's Challenge Domain

Multiplying Kobolds (F1 or F2)

You touch the stone with the emblem of the sword. Immediately you realize that Gundastav has disappeared. The Sea Sylph is missing as well and the trees look as if they have changed somehow. A clear path into the dense forest lies ahead of you at the end of the beach.

A bark, then a growl, catch your ears as a small reddish creature cautiously emerges from the trees along the path carrying a short spear.

The little beast steps into the pale moonlight, and you recognize it as a kobold.

Bravely it presses forward bearing its spear as if it will kill you all with a single stab!

The kobold is in every way a single solitary kobold. It does not speak Common and ignores any attempts to parlay in other languages. It only wishes to KILL the heroes.

If the kobold is slain with weapons or spells, it 'splits' into two kobolds who emerge from thin air to attack in the same brave manner. For each kobold killed by sword or spell, two appear to take its place. This multiplication continues until there are 100 kobolds littering the beach.

After 60 kobolds are slain in this way, the creatures stop multiplying.

If at any time a kobold is slain with fists, wrestling, or any other barehanded technique, the creature dies without multiplying.

A kobold knocked unconscious or put to sleep does not multiply. The creature must die by a non-barehanded means to multiply. Every kobold is in a state of aggressive madness when conscious and attacks by any means at its disposal.

The Best Offense (F3 or F4)

A twelve foot tall warrior, clad in plate armor so complete you are unable to discern what sort of creature is within, occupies the center of a white circle surrounded by a clearing. The large warrior shifts from side to side slightly, mist rolling from the visor when its heavy breath meets the cool air.

The circle appears to be salt granules, and it borders a fighting arena while keeping the forest at bay.

The tremendous armed warrior bears a very large nine foot high tower shield and wields a huge sickening black mace that radiates darkness in smoky wisps.

The armored warrior plants its feet firmly, bracing itself as it faces you..

The warrior *(see Appendix)* cannot be harmed by creatures outside the salt circle. Arrows or spells shot from outside the arena bounce off the armor without effect. The warrior is immune to all damage as long as it remains within the circle.

Dispersing the salt doesn't disrupt the protection immediately, though after 24 hours, the disrupted salt fails to protect the warrior. A wish or similar magic can immediately alter the protective aura.

The creature is heavy and strong, but not immovable. It resists any attempts to force it out of the protective circle, but once outside the circle, it may suffer damage from any and all attackers.

A Good Defense (F5)

You enter a large clearing strewn with pieces of stone debris. A massive boulder lies half buried in the north side of the clearing.

The boulder is a giant stone tortoise *(see Appendix)*. The tortoise attacks either when it is attacked by the party or when it notices the party.

An Immovable Object (F6)

The forest gives way to a large ravine as you walk along the path. An ugly, burly giant, brandishing a club the size of a small tree trunk, stands in front of a dilapidated bridge that spans the ravine.The giant slams his club on the ground in front of him and shouts, "Pay Brok, or Brok put you in stew!"

Brok has learned that most people wishing to cross the bridge are happy to pay him money rather than wind up in his stew pot. Brok is not very smart but has learned 100 GP is a lot of money. If the characters make Charisma [Persuade] rolls [DC 15], he allows them to pay 50 GP to cross the bridge. Brok becomes confused and angry if anyone attempts to give him anything other than gold.

The Bridge: The bridge is old and ready to fall apart at any moment. If characters attempt to cross the bridge without paying Brok his money, Brok slams his club down on the bridge's surface, doing maximum damage. The bridge has a total of 20 HP and collapses when reduced to 0.

Characters on the collapsing bridge must make a Dexterity save [DC 15] to grab onto parts of the bridge that are still anchored. Any character that fails the Dexterity save falls 20', suffering 2d6 points of damage. Characters who make the save may attempt to climb what remains of the bridge with a Strength [Athletics] check [DC 15]. Failure

indicates they too fall. Any character who falls may attempt to climb either side of the ravine with a Strength [Athletics] check [DC 10].

Treasure:

Brok has attempted to conceal his camp that lies one hundred yards into the forest, but his large size and clumsy nature has left a very noticeable trail that leads directly to his home. If the party finds Brok's camp, read the following.

As you enter a clearing you see a large cave 20' in front of you. A very large pot hangs over a wide fire pit just outside the cave mouth. Several wisps of smoke rise from the smoldering remains of the latest fire.

Characters who search the pot find that it is filled with murky, lukewarm water. The water is not hot enough to cause damage, but any character who reaches into the pot must make a Constitution save [DC 13] or contract marrow rot *(see below)*.

There is nothing of value in the pot.

When the party enters the large cave, read the following.

As you enter the dimly lit cave a strong odor assaults your senses. Bones, half-rotted animal carcasses, and other fetid things you don't wish to identify are littered about the cave. A heavy chest, battered by time, rests within an arm's reach of Brok's bedding, a large pile of animal furs on the far side of the cave.The furs are musty and moth-eaten, and thus worthless, if examined closely.

Brok's Treasure:

The large chest is locked but can be opened by the key found on Brok. It can be picked with a successful Dexterity [Sleight of Hand] check [DC 10]. The lock can also be forced open with any makeshift tool and a successful Strength check [DC 15]. Once the box is open, the following treasure is found.

360 CP
120 SP
450 GP
10 gems worth 100 GP each
Scroll of Light
Potion of Healing
Armor of the Battlefield *(see Appendix)*

Marrow Rot: Marrow rot is a disease contracted when careless folk handle meat or bones that have been left to stew in too low a temperature. This disease is found most commonly in the food of creatures who regularly eat cooked humanoid flesh.

The disease takes 1d6 days to incubate. After incubation, it causes characters to feel exhausted and reduces Constitution by 1 point. Afflicted characters do not gain any benefit from short rests and only gain half benefits from long rests.

After each long rest the character must make a new Constitution saving throw [DC 10] or suffer another point of Constitution damage. If the saving throw is successful for three consecutive days, the character's body is considered to have fought off the disease. A disease-free character regains Constitution points at a rate of 1 per every long rest.

An Unstoppable Force

The following encounter can occur at any time the GM wishes. When the GM chooses to use this encounter, read the following.

The ground around you trembles slightly as a massive mound of earth juts out of the ground in front of you. In a matter of moments, the mound takes the form of a half-formed humanoid. The strange creature made of earth roars in anger, a sound more like grating boulders, and closes to attack.

The creature is an earth elemental (MM pg. 124), and it gains a surprise round. The elemental fights until it is reduced to half HP. When this occurs, it melds back into the earth to flee. The elemental bides its time until the party is weakened in some way and then attacks again at an inopportune moment of the GM's choosing. The second time the elemental attacks the party, it fights until dead or the party is vanquished.

The Vestiges of Lunacy

The final part of the Fighter's Challenge takes place in the area on the map marked "Vestiges of Lunacy". This area was at one time, a massive outdoor temple complex devoted to a long-forgotten god of insanity. Over the years, the Vestiges of lunacy have housed a variety of would-be cult leaders, ruthless warlords, and more. Five years ago, a medusa discovered this area and decided it would make a perfect place for her lair. In that time, she worked on decorating the vestiges with a variety of her works of art.

Recently a band of hobgoblins also happened upon the Vestiges of lunacy. The medusa tried to fight them, but found herself their prisoner instead. The hobgoblins were preparing to kill the medusa, but she managed to turn their shaman into a stone statue during the battle. The tribe is currently trying to force her to return the shaman to his normal form.

Arriving at the Vestiges

When the party arrives at the area on the map for the vestiges, read the following.

You break from the woods that have surrounded you for most of the journey and see a large field with dozens of ruins scattered about the ground. In the distance, a mound reaches several yards into the air.

As the party enters the area of the Vestiges of Lunacy, roll 1d6 once every hour of game time. A 1 indicates an encounter occurs with a patrol of 2d4 hobgoblins.

Not counting the chief and his retinue, there are 40 hobgoblins in total. This number includes both random encounters and planned encounters. As the party dispatches each hobgoblin, adjust the total. If the total drops to 0, then no more random encounters occur while the characters explore the Vestiges of Lunacy.

Treasure: Each hobgoblin encountered has 1d8 CP, 1d6 SP, and 1d4 GP in its possession.

Ambush

Six hobgoblins (MM pg. 186) are very well hidden among the ruins. A Perception check [DC 20] is required to notice them. If the party does not spot the hobgoblins, they attack once anyone in the party is within 20'. They attack with a volley of longbow arrows, followed by engaging in melee.

Treasure: Each hobgoblin encountered will have 1d8 CP, 1d6 SP, and 1d4 GP in its possession.

The Mound

The mound is 50' and 200' across high with a level top. When the Temple of Lunacy was constructed, the top of the mound was flattened, and a long set of stairs was built into its side. Both the temple and the long stairs have fallen into disrepair.

Characters attempting to climb the mound may use the ancient stairs. Doing so does not require a skill check of any kind but approaching without stealth can alert the hobgoblins at the top of the mound. If a character chooses to climb the mound without using the stairs, a Strength [Athletics] check [DC 10] is required. Failure indicates a loss of footing.

Any character who loses footing begins rolling downhill, taking 1d4 HP of bludgeoning damage until either making a Dexterity save [DC 10] or reaching the bottom of the mound.

The Throne of Sharanda

As you crest the top of the hill, the flat mesa is littered with the ruins of ancient stone works. Several statues stand scattered throughout the ruins. A grand throne stands prominently in the center of the mesa, a large boulder behind it.

A brutish hobgoblin sits upon the throne and yanks on the chains of a bound woman whose head has been covered with a sack. The woman is struggling desperately against the chains. Several hobgoblins surround the area to ensure she does not escape.

As the characters make their way toward the throne, allow them each a passive Perception check [DC 10] to notice that most of the statues are not only very well made, but also appear to be quite new in relation to the age of the ruins around them. This can give them a clue as to the captive's identity.

The hobgoblin on the throne is the hobgoblin leader (Hobgoblin Captain MM pg. 186). His attention is focused solely on the prisoner. The 6 hobgoblins near the hobgoblin captain find tormenting their prisoner far more entertaining than keeping an eye out for strangers and are at a -4 penalty on passive Perception checks.

Once the heroes have defeated the hobgoblins, they may remove the sack that covers the captive woman's head. When they do so, they discover that the captive is a medusa (MM pg. 214).

The Barracks

The hobgoblins built this makeshift camp to serve as a barracks for themselves. Two guards stand at the entrance of the barracks, but there is no other attempt at security.

The hobgoblins send out patrols on a routine basis. At any time there are 2d8 hobgoblins in the barracks. Half of any hobgoblins within the barracks area are sleeping.

If combat begins, the GM should roll a 1d6; a result of a 1 indicates a patrol of 2d4 hobgoblins has heard the fighting and arrives to enter the fray within 1d6 rounds.

Treasure:

Each hobgoblin encountered will have 1d8 CP, 1d6 SP, and 1d4 GP in its possession.

Cleric's Challenge

The medusa attempts to parley with the heroes. She wants nothing more than to be left alone. If the party does engage in conversation with the medusa, she offers to reverse the petrification of any party member who has become petrified. She also offers up the location of her hidden treasure.

If the party chooses not to engage in diplomacy with the medusa, they may still find the treasure with a successful Perception check [DC 15]. The treasure is hidden in a secret compartment under the throne and contains the following treasure.

450 CP
230 SP
145 GP
4 Potions of Turn Stone to Flesh
1 Scroll of Feather Fall
+2 Longsword

The boulder behind the chair is a teleportation stone. Any character touching it will be transported back to the beginning island beach of the Marathon of Heroes.

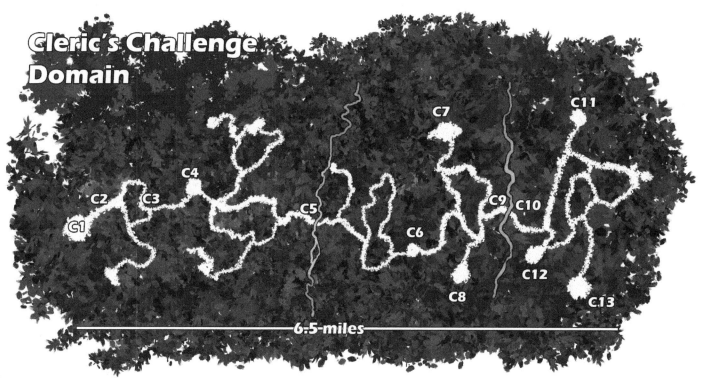

Cleric's Challenge Domain

6.5 miles

The Domain

The cleric's challenge is a 6.5-mile journey in which the cleric is required to use divine energy to power each of six beacons. Each beacon is one mile apart from the others and features a challenge requiring the cleric to use unique skills and abilities to succeed.

As the cleric activates each beacon, a horde of undead is kept at bay. Each beacon has a secondary ability that remains active until the next beacon is activated.

During this challenge banals who attempt to fly can do so no longer than 2 rounds before they find themselves exhausted and in a random part of the forest. Attempts at teleportation simply do not work.

The proximity of the Chaos Void causes all characters to suffer a hit point penalty of -1 per character level, and all saving throws are made at -1. Clerics make all Turn Undead checks at one level above their current character level, and all divine spells, regardless of class, are cast at one level higher.

The PCs will encounter patches of Mists of Lunacy throughout this challenge *(see Mists of Lunacy section)*. If a character falls prey to the mist's insanity, consult the following table.

Sanity Effects of the Mists (Cleric's Challenge)	
1	Becomes a pacifist and does not attack monsters for lethal damage.
2	Delusions of Grandeur – Insists on being the party leader and becomes hostile if commands are not followed.
3	Looks like a zombie to everyone else.
4	Believes the party must be sacrificed to appease the god of mists.
5	Better me than you – Attempts to cripple another party member to slow the horde's pursuit as it stops to feed on the victim.
6	Hallucinations – Sees ghosts on the path and attempts to avoid them.

Beacon of Protection (C1)

You reach out and touch the stone with the star burnt into its surface. You find yourself standing in a forest clearing roughly thirty feet in diameter. A 6' tall crystal pyramid stands in the middle of the clearing. The pyramid is 10' wide at its base and covered in strange markings. A narrow footpath leads east from the clearing into the dark and tangled forest surrounding you. As you adjust to your new surroundings the markings on the pyramid begin to move, forming the phrase "Faith or Blood" before dissolving back into undecipherable scribbles.

Allow the characters two rounds to explore their surroundings (described in features) before reading the following.

As you explore your new surroundings you hear the moans and shuffling movements of many creatures.

Anyone succeeding on a Perception check [DC 10] can see that dozens of shambling creatures are making their way out of the forest. An appropriate Intelligence [Knowledge] check (such as religion or monsters) reveals that the creatures are zombies. Due to the slow speed of the zombies and the difficult terrain they are traveling through, players have two rounds before the zombies are close enough to engage in melee.

If Detect Magic is used, the pyramid radiates small amounts of positive energy.

If at any time a cleric uses the channel divinity ability to Turn Undead *or* the party suffers a total of 15 HP points of damage read the following.

The crystal bursts with light, surrounding you in a glow of warmth and safety. A rush of holy energy streaks from the tip of the pyramid, striking all the zombies within 20' and destroying them instantly. The army of zombies outside the radius of the glow stops moving and is kept at bay by the energy emanating from the crystal.

Each character is now surrounded by an aura of divine energy that extends in a 12' radius. This aura extends in a sphere and moves with the character. This energy keeps the undead at bay and suspends the -1 HP per level penalty. Both effects last for one hour.

If the party does not reach the next beacon before the aura extinguishes, each character loses 1 HP per level and suffers a second HP per level penalty, and the zombies begin attacking. 1d6 zombies per round can get close enough to engage in melee.

Through the Forest (C2)

If the party follows the path leading from the clearing, begin tracking time the moment they are 30' away from any activated pyramid. At first, the aura surrounding each character is very strong. However, as time goes by, a successful Perception check [DC 15] reveals that the aura is fading at the rate of 2' per ten minutes. As the aura fades the endless horde of zombies press closer. They cannot enter the aura unless forced to do so. If protected characters approach a zombie, the creature attempts to move away from the character by any means at its disposal.

The path through the forest is well worn. Aside from planned obstacles and encounters, the party can travel at a speed of at least 3 MPH without checking for exhaustion. If a character attempts to travel through the forest, the dense vegetation reduces all movement to slow movement. Due to the dense overgrowth, all non-piercing attacks are made at a -2 penalty.

Overgrown Vegetation (C3)

After the party travels about half a mile through the forest, read the following.

As you travel through the forest, the sound of the endless horde of zombies just beyond the radius of the divine energy that surrounds you is a constant reminder that you cannot dally. You take a turn on the path to confront a mass of tangled and overgrown vegetation 20' ahead.

A shambling mound has made its home within the mass of vegetation (MM pg. 270).

Keep in mind that the radius of the divine aura surrounding each member has receded at a rate of 2' per every ten minutes and that the horde of undead press as close as they can during this encounter.

The Second Beacon (C4)

You have traveled 1 mile since you left the comfort of the crystal pyramid when you arrive at another clearing. This clearing is 30' in diameter and much like the first. A 6' tall crystal pyramid with a 10' base stands in the center.

If any of the aura remains when the party arrives, the beacon absorbs what is left and once again surrounds each character in a 12' radius of divine energy. If the aura has faded away, the party must recharge the beacon with either a cleric using channel divine energy (Turn Undead), or by suffering 15 HP worth of damage.

The primary effect of the protection aura remains the same, but the secondary effect fades. The penalty on saving throws is removed while the aura is active, but the HP penalty of -1 per level remains active. The divine aura fades at a rate of 2' per ten minutes once a character is beyond 30' of the pyramid.

River (C5)

As the party approaches area 5 on the map, read the following.

You have heard rushing water for several minutes before arriving on the banks of a swiftly moving river. The river flows from the north of the forest and continues its journey south before disappearing into the darkness of the dense forest. From the banks of the river you can tell that the current is very strong.

The river is about 15' wide and 4' deep at the deepest point. Any character who looks across the river and succeeds at a Perception check [DC 10] notices that zombies do not appear to be on the other side. Remaining in contact with the river pulls at banal sanity. Every round in the water requires a WIS check [DC 15] or suffer 1d4 damage to sanity. Ingesting the water is an automatic failure to save.

Characters attempting to cross the river on foot must make Strength [Athletics] checks [DC 15] or be swept away by the current. This check is modified by -1 for each size category below medium and +1 for each size category above medium. If a character uses a rope that is anchored by either another character or something such as a tree, the saving roll is at advantage.

If a character is swept away by the current, a Strength [Athletics] check [DC 20] must be made to swim or begin drowning (use rules for suffocation located in PHB pg. 183). If the character is tied to a rope, the DC for the Strength [Athletics] check is made at advantage. If a character is swimming, an attempt to regain footing can be made with a Strength [Athletics] check [DC 15] at disadvantage.

Once the party makes its way across the river, read the following.

You have made your way across the river and now stand on the opposite bank. There appears to be no sign of the zombie horde. The path you have been following continues to wind in between the trees but becomes impossible to see once it crosses into a thick mist.

The mists ahead are Mists of Lunacy. If the characters are surrounded by the divine aura, they don't need to make a saving throw vs. the mists. Any character that does not have darkvision is unable to see more than 10' in any direction and cannot move at fast speed without the risk of getting lost [Wisdom check DC 15].

Anyone in the mists not surrounded by the divine aura must make Intelligence saving throws DC 15 or lose 1d4 points of Sanity. Any character that becomes insane needs to roll on the affliction table at the beginning of this challenge.

Beacon of Light (C6)

You press through the mists, arriving at another pyramid. Just like the others, it is 6' in height with a base of 10'. The clearing appears to be empty other than the pyramid and the mist that has been your companion since you left the banks of the river.

The clearing is empty save for the pyramid. As with the other pyramids, if the aura is still active, the pyramid absorbs any remaining divine energy and recharges the aura around each character. If the aura has faded away from any character, a channel divine energy (Turn Undead) or the loss of a total of 15 HP causes the pyramid to glow and once again surrounds each character in divine aura. The secondary effect of this pyramid grants all characters darkvision.

Owlbear's Den (C7)

Once the party leaves the 30' zone around the third beacon, the Game Master should roll a 1d10 every 10 minutes of game time. A result of 1–3 means that the pair of owlbears who lair nearby have picked up the scent of the party and are stalking them. Once detected, the two owlbears attack in 1d4 rounds. Allow each character to make appropriate Perception checks to determine if they are surprised by the owlbears. (Information for owlbears MM pg. 250.)

If the adventurers defeat the owlbears, they can search for the beasts, den. If they do so, make the appropriate Tracking checks. Success indicates the party finds the den in 1d6x3 minutes. Within the lair, the following treasure lies amongst the discarded bones of past victims.

250 GP
135 SP
Two Potions of Cure Light Wounds
Ring of Protection +1
Mace +2/+4 vs. Dragons

Beacon of Rest (C8)

You arrive at a clearing where again you see a pyramid. There appears to be nothing but the pyramid and low ground fog here, much like the mists you have seen before.

The clearing is empty save for the pyramid. As with other pyramids, if the party is still surrounded by the divine aura, the pyramid absorbs what remains and recharges the aura around each character. If the aura has faded away, then channel divine energy (Turn Undead) or the loss of a total of 15 HP causes the pyramid to glow and once again surround each character in a divine aura. The secondary effect of charging this beacon grants each character the effects of a short rest (PHB pg. 186). The mists are not mind-altering, it is only ground fog.

Another River to Cross (C9)

You arrive on the banks of a 20' wide river that flows lazily from the north to the south. You can see where several large trees have been knocked over, creating a natural bridge across the river.

An ochre jelly (MM pg. 244) clings to the bottom of the tree bridge, attacking anyone attempting to cross. During the encounter, anyone struck by the jelly while still on the bridge must make a Dexterity check [DC 15] or fall into the river. Victims in the river are attacked by a grey ooze (MM pg. 224) that lies in wait in the water under the bridge.

After the encounter, any character diving to the bottom of the river (5' deep) can make Perception checks each round with the following results (note: each result can only occur once).

DC 10 – 3d10 CP
DC 15 – 2d10 SP
DC 20 – Chainmail +1

Beyond the River (C10)

Once the party makes its way across the river, things change a little. The beacons have been destroyed by the pack of werewolves that call this section of the forest its home. Along with the loss of any benefits from the pyramids, the party runs the risk of being detected by a werewolf and becoming hunted. While the party should be able to easily deal with 1–2 werewolves, if the entire pack is on its trail, a desperate race to the end of this leg of the Marathon of Heroes begins.

Once the PCs travel beyond the river, the Game Master should roll 1d10 once every ten minutes. On a result of

1, a werewolf detects the party and will attempt to sneak closer to it in order to assess its strength. If the werewolf is detected, the party can choose to engage in combat. The werewolf's first action when combat begins is to howl and summon nearby pack mates. If the werewolf lets out a howl, it alerts 1d4 werewolves who arrive in 1d6 rounds.

If the party defeats the summoned werewolves, return to making checks on a 1d10 every ten minutes. Continue this process until the party reaches the end of the challenge or until a total of 20 werewolves have been killed.

The Fifth/Sixth Beacon (C11 & C12)

As the characters approach the fifth and sixth beacon, read the following.

As you arrive at another 30' diameter clearing in the forest you see that instead of a pyramid the ground is littered with shattered crystal.

These pyramids have been destroyed by the pack of werewolves that now call this area home. If a character investigates the broken shards, allow them a Perception check [DC 20] to discover that many of the shards have been scarred with claw marks from a powerful beast. A successful Intelligence check [DC 20] reveals that these claw marks were more than likely made by a large wolf.

Lair of the Wolf Lord (C13)

This location is the lair of the werewolf pack, and the party must face off against the leader of the pack known as the wolf lord. The wolf lord is a massive ogre named Grush *(see Appendix)* who was infected with lycanthropy several years ago and has since formed quite a large pack.

To complete this challenge, the party must touch the stone that is within the confines of the werewolf lair. As the party enters the lair, read the following.

> You enter a large cavern opening and immediately smell the scent of the many werewolves who call this lair home. As your eyes adjust to the darkness of the cavern you see a massive form squatting in the middle of the cave. The beast looks at you and lets out a howl when it races to attack you.

If Grush is defeated, any surviving werewolves decide to flee the area. The party is free to search the cave as well as touch the stone to return to the beginning of the marathon. If the cave is searched, the party finds the following treasure.

23 PP, 156 GP, 345 SP
1 small sapphire worth 50 GP
2 large rubies worth 100 GP each
2 Scrolls of Cure Disease
1 Scroll of Remove Curse
Helm of Wisdom +2

Wizard's Challenge

The Domain

This challenge ends when the characters reach a shrine located at the opposite side of a 6.5-mile-wide ravine. Most of this challenge takes place as the characters navigate their way over a deep and seemingly endless ravine. Fly and levitation only work correctly in specific areas, otherwise the penalties described in the Fighter's Challenge also apply here. As with other challenges in the marathon, once this challenge is finished, the characters are transported back to the start of the marathon to choose the next stage of their journey.

In the Wizard's Challenge, arcane casters cast all spells at one level above their current level. This does not grant extra spells or abilities, it only changes the effects of spells cast. All combat rolls are made at -1, and all healing spells also suffer a -1 per hit die penalty.

During the Wizard's Challenge it is possible for a character to come into contact with the Mists of Lunacy. Consult the beginning of this module for rules on how the mists work. If a character suffers a lunacy effect while participating in the Wizard's Challenge, use the following table.

Sanity Effects of the Mists (Wizard's Challenge)	
1	Character believes to be an ogre.
2	Character randomly barks while speaking.
3	Character's eyes change colors dramatically every 1d6 hours.
4	Character believes to be a criminal mastermind intent on victimizing the other party members.
5	One leg grows one foot longer than the other, forcing the character to move at slow speed.
6	Fingers become tentacles. -1 on skill checks that require hands.

The ravine is one mile deep and filled with mists that slowly drive any character (foolish enough to spend longer than a round immersed in the depths) insane.

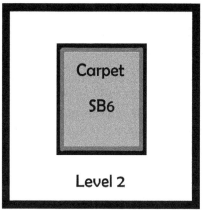

A Misty Ravine

You touch the stone with the emblem of the fireball and find yourself standing on the edge of a massive ravine. The ravine is so wide that you can't see the other side. Looking down, the ravine is filled with a roiling mist like that which has surrounded the island since your arrival. Nearby is a six-foot-high, three-foot-wide ancient stone monolith, its engravings obscured with pock marks and scratches.

There are several options available to the players but the one that yields the most significant result is using Comprehend Languages on the stone. Time has worn away a lot of the writing engraved on the stone but there is still enough left that a character using Comprehend Languages is able to determine that the gist of the writing is "going up".

If the characters attempt to explore the edge of the ravine, they find the terrain is incredibly difficult to traverse, reducing all movement by half. If the characters continue traveling along the edge of the ravine for more than 10 rounds, fierce winds begin slowing their movement down to ¼ normal speed. After 15 rounds, the Mists of Lunacy arrive, forcing the characters to begin saving throws or suffer the effects of growing lunacy.

If the players are truly foolhardy, they may decide to have their characters attempt to climb down the ledge. If this happens, the first ten feet of the climb is relatively easy. However, once the characters are immersed in the mists, the climb becomes much more difficult. Along with the climb being more difficult, the characters must also contend with the Mists of Lunacy.

Do You Think You Can Fly?

If the characters correctly assume the message on the stone means they should fly up, they need a character capable of casting the Fly or Levitate spell. If the arcane caster of the group does not have the Fly spell prepared, they may take the time to prepare it at the location of the stone without risk of being attacked. If for some reason the arcane caster in the group does not have the Fly spell, the GM may inform that along with the directions of "going up" the ancient stone has the Fly spell engraved on its surface.

Because the Wizard's Challenge allows all arcane spells to be cast at one level higher, it is possible for a fifth level wizard to cast Fly on up to four people. If the party consists of more than four people, a little bit of creativity should still allow for the entire party to travel by means of the Fly spell.

Once the Fly spell has been cast, the party quickly learns that they cannot travel farther than 10 feet from the base of the stone before the spell begins to disperse and they start to fall. They must fly straight upwards. As the party reaches 500' in elevation, read the following.

You fly upwards. After 500 feet, the unlikely sight of a large stone block emerges just above you. You estimate this block of stone measures about 50' wide, 50' deep, and 30' feet tall. There is a six-foot-tall, three-foot-wide arched opening in the center of the base of the stone block's south side.

The Stone Block

Once the characters are within 10' of the stone block they may investigate the outside of the object. If they choose to do so, they find nothing of interest other than the opening. Once they enter the opening of the stone block, read the following.

You find yourself in a 10' wide, 10' high stone corridor that leads into an unnatural darkness.

The Game Master should refer to the map at the beginning of the section for details on each entry. The stone block is an ancient structure that houses a unique Flying Carpet. The party can use the carpet to travel the remaining distance of this leg of the Marathon of Heroes. To gain access to the Flying Carpet, the party must first solve the puzzle of the first level. The stairs in the north section of SB1 are not visible or detectable until the puzzle in SB5 is resolved.

The stone block has the following features unless otherwise noted. While the party is within the confines of dark stone passages, natural light sources function at half radius, while magical light sources produce light at double the normal radius.

Unless the Game Master decides otherwise, the stone block does not have any monster encounters. This allows the party to take its time within the structure and gives arcane spell casters the opportunity to regain used spells or to prepare the spells that are required to solve the puzzle. If for some reason the arcane caster either does not possess or cannot cast the required spells, repeating the phrase "going up" summons a large disc 20' in diameter. If a character steps on the disc, it raises up to the entry.

SB1

This cross-shaped room is empty of everything save small amounts of debris that have gathered here over time. A look at the map reveals this room is used to gain access to rooms SB2–5. The way to attain entry into each room is described in each room's entry below.

SB2

When the south side of this room is inspected, a Perception check [DC 5] reveals a small crack in the wall. If investigated further, a Perception check [DC 15] detects a faint breeze coming from the crack. The crack in this wall is the only way to gain access to the room beyond. Characters will need to alter their form in some way to enter through the crack. While Gaseous Form is probably the easiest way to enter this room, Game Masters should feel free to adjudicate other actions as they deem fit.

If the party does not have someone capable of casting Gaseous Form, they can enter the room by forcing the crack wider. To do this a character may attack the wall. Blunt weapons do full damage, while slashing and piercing weapons only do half damage. Once the wall has suffered 50 points of damage, the crack is wide enough for a medium sized character to squeeze through. Once a character enters the room, read the following.

As you make your way through the crack in the wall you find yourself in a 20' by 20' square room that is empty save for a small stone pillar, about two feet high and one foot in diameter, topped with a dull yellowish gem.

This room is empty except for the small pillar. If the pillar is investigated closer, read the following.

The stone pillar is unremarkable in all ways. The gem on top of the pillar is obviously dull and of little value. However, as you inspect the gem closer you notice that a hand surrounded by what appears to be a burst of electricity has been etched on the gem's surface.

Any character within the room is free to attempt to pry the gem loose, but these attempts fail as an arcane force holds the gem to the pillar. If a character touches the gem while using the spell Shocking Grasp, or in some other way imbues the gem with an electric charge (such as with a strike from flint and steel), a grinding sound can be heard as part of the east wall descends beneath the surface of the room revealing a doorway. After this event, a similar grinding can be heard as the south wall of SB3 reveals a doorway in the same fashion.

SB3

When someone enters the room of SB3, read the following.

A torch about 5 feet in height and topped with a strong flame juts from the center of the room, shedding light that reveals the room to be otherwise empty. The heat radiated by the torch feels warm upon your face.

The heat created by the torch is not harmful but can make a character uncomfortable if they stay in the room too long. The uncomfortable heat causes a -1 cumulative effect on skill checks for every five rounds spent in the room. The torch itself is safe to touch. However, touching the flame will cause 1d4 points of burning damage each round of contact.

The "key" to the puzzle in this room is to extinguish the flame. This can be accomplished through magical means such as the use of a Ray of Frost spell or similar cold-based spell. If a character attempts to smother the flame with an object, the object suffers 1d4 points of damage per round. If the object is held against the flame for 4 rounds the flame extinguishes.

Once the flame is extinguished, a grinding noise is heard, and a doorway in the north wall of SB4 is revealed.

SB4

Cold begins to grip you in its icy embrace as you enter this 20' by 20' square room. In its center, a pillar of ice extends from floor to ceiling.

The cold in this room is not directly harmful. However, after five rounds any character that does not leave the room suffers a -1 on all skill checks. This effect is cumulative for every five rounds spent inside the room (-2 on skill checks after 10 rounds, -3 after 15 rounds, etc.). Once a character leaves the room, they regain lost points at a rate of 1 point per every three rounds spent outside the room.

Characters investigating the pillar of ice may roll a Perception check [DC 10]. Success reveals a lever trapped in the ice. The ice can be melted by mundane means by holding some form of flame (such as that created by a torch) for 4 rounds. A character using a fire-based spell causes the ice to melt in 1 round. Once the ice is melted, the lever can be pulled with little effort.

If the lever in the floor is pulled, a grinding sound is heard and an entry into SB5 is revealed.

SB5

This 20' by 20' square room appears to be completely empty.

This room is not as empty as it appears. An invisible lever, similar to the one found in SB4, hides in the center of the room. Spells such as See Invisibility reveal the lever. Any character that uses hands or an object around the lever has a 50% chance per round to detect the lever as well.

When the lever is pulled, it activates a set of stairs hidden in the northern ceiling of SB1. This stairway leads to SB6.

SB6

As you ascend the stairs you enter a large 30' by 30' square room that is devoid of any decorations other than a large 20' by 20' carpet on the floor. A slight draft of wind is felt coming from the north.

This room is empty other than the large carpet on the floor in the center of the room. Anyone who investigates the carpet may roll a Perception check [DC 15] to notice that the carpet hovers slightly above the floor. If anyone stands on the carpet, it continues to hover.

The use of Detect Magic reveals the carpet emanates a strong transmutation aura. This carpet is a special Flying Carpet meant to be used by the party to finish this leg of the Marathon of Heroes.

The magic carpet is not a normal magic carpet. The carpet only moves north or south. It does not go up, down, east, or west. Anyone in control of the carpet can adjust the carpet's speed between 0' and 120' per round. The carpet continues to move provided it has enough spell energy to do so. The carpet flies for one hour per every arcane spell level cast into the carpet. 0 level spells count for half a spell level. Divine magic can also power the carpet but takes two spell levels per hour.

If anyone investigates the north wall, they discover that the wall is an illusion. Detect Magic reveals that strong illusion magic permeates the wall. The wall can be passed through and serves as the departure point for the magic carpet. Once the group figures out how the carpet works and leaves the stone block, they begin the final and longest leg of this part of the marathon.

Come with Me on a Magic Carpet Ride

Because the magic carpet flies, there are several chances for encounters with a variety of flying monsters. There are no keyed encounters for the next 6.5 miles, but the Game Master should check for random encounters once every mile. Roll a d6; a result of 1 results in an encounter. See table WC1 to determine the encounter.

If the GM prefers not to use random encounters, feel free to use the table below to plan a few encounters or create your own. It is suggested that the party have at least 2 encounters during this leg of the journey.

WC1: Encounters on the Magic Carpet Ride	
1	Wyvern (MM pg. 303)
2	2d4 Harpies (MM pg. 181)
3	Air Elemental (MM pg. 124)
4	1d3 Manticore (MM pg. 213)
5	Blue Dragon Wyrmling (MM pg. 91)
6	1d4 Peryton (MM pg. 251)
7	Chimera (MM pg. 39)
8	1d4 Griffons (MM pg. 174)
9	1d4 Flying Swords (MM pg. 20)
10	1d3 Gargoyles (MM pg. 140)

End of the Line

At the end of the 6.5 mile ride, the magic carpet comes to a stop on a 50' by 50' platform. The platform is home to 6 harpies who attack the characters once they are within 100 yards of their nesting site. After the characters arrive at the platform and have dispatched the harpies, read the following.

There is a large platform ahead of you. As you approach the platform, the carpet slows until it comes to a complete stop and remains hovering a few inches above the stone. Several large nests have been constructed on the platform, and an unpleasant order permeates the entire area.

A search of the nests provides the following treasure.

459 CP
342 SP
115 GP
12 PP
Two Potions of Feather Fall
One Scroll of Firebolt
Robes of the Red Dragon Mage *(see Appendix)*

This platform hovers 500' above the ground and requires the players to devise some method of getting down to the ground below. Once the characters are on the ground, there is a stone like the ones at the beginning of the Marathon of Heroes. Touching this stone takes them back to the beginning of the marathon where they can choose which leg of the journey they wish to attempt next.

Rogue's Challenge

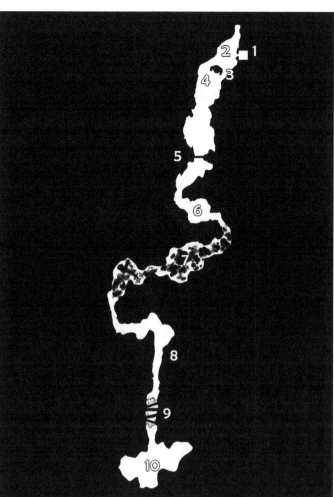

The Domain

This challenge ends at the center of the island after the party has traveled along a 6.5-mile-long canyon that begins in the north of the island and expands southward. The party faces off against several challenges that are designed to allow rogues to showcase their talents. Success can be had without the presence of a rogue in the party, even though the Rogue's Challenge is designed with rogues in mind. This challenge tests both the wits and combat capability of the party and requires players to make split second decisions.

Fly spells and Levitation have limited effect while in the canyon, each lasting only two rounds before ending. Characters in the canyon suffer -1 to all saving throws, but sneak attacks gain a +1 bonus to both attack and damage rolls.

The canyon is filled with the Mists of Lunacy starting ten feet above the floor of the canyon and ending near the invisible top. When exposed to the mists, player characters must make an INT save [DC 15] or suffer 1d4 points of Sanity damage. Those so affected have an additional 50% chance of suffering effects from the afflictions table that follows.

Sanity Effects of the Mists (Rogue's Challenge)	
1	Kleptomania – The character feels a need to steal treasure from other players.
2	Avarice – The character becomes obsessed with saving money.
3	Hair Stylist – The character's hair changes color and style every few minutes.
4	Living Nightmare – The character believes to be in a nightmare and tries to wake up every 1d6 hours by laying down and standing back up, slapping face, etc...
5	Enraged – Character only engages monsters and other threats in melee.
6	Depression – Character does not receive advantage dice.

1d12 Sanity points can be cured in this domain with a Remove Curse spell.

1: Rats in a cage

When the characters touch the stone with the key, read the following.

You reach out and touch the stone with the key symbol and find yourself in a 10' by 10' room with only a bound oak door set in the east wall.

The only way out of the room is through the door in the east wall. It is locked but can be opened a number of ways. Any character with a set of thieves' tools can attempt to pick the lock with a Dexterity [Sleight of Hand] [DC 15] check. The door can be forced open with a Strength check [DC 20]. A spell such as Knock also opens the door.

2: Enter the Juggernaut

As the characters exit the room, read the following.

You exit the room and find yourself standing in a twenty-foot wide canyon. The Mists of Lunacy swirl 10' above you. The back of a large statue can be seen twenty feet in front of you, its head brushing the bottom of the mists that act as a strange ceiling for the canyon.

The statue is a clay golem (MM pg. 169) that does not activate unless a character moves in front of it. If a character moves in front of the golem, read entry 3.

Characters may attempt to climb the canyon walls on either side. A successful Strength [Athletics] check [DC 15] means they succeed. If characters climb 10' or higher, they must begin making Intelligence [DC 15] saves or suffer 1d4 points of Sanity loss. The canyon walls are over 200' high and require an Intelligence [DC 15] save and a Strength [Athletics] [DC 15] check every 10'. If characters make it to the top of the canyon wall, they find themselves in an unknown part of the island. This goes beyond the scope of this adventure, thus Game Masters have the responsibility of refereeing anything beyond what is contained therein.

3: The Unstoppable Juggernaut

If a character passes the location of the clay golem, read the following.

A booming voice reverberates through the canyon when you pass the motionless statue.

"Flee for your lives like the rats you are!"

The clay statue begins to move by taking a step forward.

Allow the players one round of action before rolling initiative. The clay golem begins attacking anyone within range. If nothing is within range, it pursues the nearest character.

It should be noted that destroying the clay golem is unlikely or extremely difficult. Running from it is probably the best option. If the players decide to stand to fight the clay golem, run the encounter as normal. If the players decide to run, move onto section 4.

4: An Unstoppable Force

The characters should easily outpace the ponderous clay golem. However, the golem will continue its pursuit relentlessly, even as characters stop to deal with obstacles. For this reason, it is imperative the Game Master keep track of everyone's location to know how much of a lead each character has on the clay golem as they approach each obstacle.

One way to keep track of things is to have each PC roll a Strength [Athletics] check [DC 10]. A success indicates the PC is one round ahead of the golem, while a failure indicates the golem has caught up to the character by one round. While the Game Master is welcome to require this check as often as wished, only one Strength [Athletics] check per half-mile is recommended (approximately twice between each obstacle).

Each success is cumulative. Thus, a character who scores two successes in a row would be two rounds ahead of the golem. As with successes, each failure is cumulative as well. A character with two failures in a row allows the golem to catch up by two rounds. If a character ever accrues more failures than successes, this means the golem has caught up to the character and attacks. However, a character who is attacked by the golem does not have to stand to fight; they are welcome to once again run and continue making checks as described above or seek other solutions.

During the chase, there are several times where characters may be required to slow down to negotiate a challenge. When this happens, keep track of how many rounds the characters spend dealing with the obstacles and allow the golem to gain that many rounds on the party.

If the golem catches up to a character while attempting to negotiate an obstacle, it attacks as normal until the character is either able to escape or the golem goes berserk.

If the golem ever goes berserk (as described in the MM entry pg. 169), it stops chasing the characters and blindly attacks the canyon walls for 1d4 rounds before resuming the chase. Each attack causes debris to fall into the canyon, requiring each character to make a Dexterity [Acrobatics] check [DC 10] or suffer 1d6 points of damage from being pelted with falling debris. While berserk, the golem automatically fails Dexterity checks and suffers 1d6 points of damage each round it pounds at the canyon walls.

5: Tripwire

When characters approach area 5, they must make a Perception check [DC 10]. Keep in mind that if they are running, they are only allowed a passive Perception check unless they have an ability that negates this penalty.

If characters succeed on the Perception check, they see a tripwire stretched across the bottom of the canyon only a couple of inches above the canyon floor. The tripwire is easy to step over but doing so costs one round of movement.

The tripwire sets off a rockslide causing 1d10 points [Dexterity save DC 15 for half] of damage to any character within 10' of the location.

Disarming the trap requires an Intelligence check [DC 15] to learn that tripping the wire sets off a rockslide. If a character with thieves' tools succeeds on a Dexterity check [DC 15], the trap is disarmed. If the character fails on the Dexterity check, the rockslide occurs, causing 1d10 points of damage to anyone within 10' of the tripwire.

If the trap is not disarmed and the characters all choose to simply step over the tripwire, the golem has a 30% chance of triggering the trap when it arrives at the location.

6: False Ground

When a characters come within sixty feet of this location, allow them to make Perception checks [DC 20]. A success reveals that the floor of the canyon is unusual. Any character that makes an Intelligence [Nature] check [DC 15] discerns that this is the lair of a giant trap door spider *(see Appendix)* and that anyone within 10' of the entry risks attack.

Any character who does not wish to fight the spider with the golem closing the distance may attempt a Strength [Athletics] check [DC 15] to scale the walls. PCs manage to avoid alerting the spider to their presence on a successful check. If this check is failed, the character falls from the cliff side, suffering 1d6 points of damage and alerting the spider.

If the spider is defeated, a character may enter its lair. A Dexterity check [DC 10] is required to navigate the earthen tunnel without getting stuck in strands of the spider webbing. A character stuck in webbing must make a Strength check [DC 15] or devise a solution to break free. Any character making it to the bottom of the ten-foot-long tunnel will find the following items belonging to past victims of the spider.

400 CP
150 SP
60 GP
Potion of Healing
Potion of Climbing
+1 Leather Armor of Nimble Skills *(see Appendix)*

When the golem reaches this area, if the spider is still alive, the golem loses two rounds in the chase as it combats the giant arachnid.

Clever PCs may elude the golem with the use of the spider lair or other means. The rogue leading the party may have numerous solutions to kill, distract, or incapacitate the creature. Successful clever attempts to thwart the brute should be rewarded.

7: Rubble in the Way

Once a character comes within sixty feet of this location, read the following.

> A large field of rubble comes into view ahead when you round a small bend in the seemingly endless canyon. From your location, the rubble looks passable.

The field of rubble covers the width of the canyon floor and extends for the next ½ mile.

The rubble can be easily navigated without a skill check if a character moves at slow speed. This does allow the golem to gain on the party, but assures the characters cross without harm. If the characters choose to move at normal speed, they must make a Dexterity [Acrobatics] [DC 15] check or fall, suffering 1d4 points of damage. A character only needs to succeed on a single skill check to move across the whole field without falling. If moving at fast speed, the character must succeed at a Dexterity [Acrobatics] [DC 20] check or fall, suffering 1d6 points of damage. A character only needs to succeed once to be able to move through the rubble at fast speed without falling. A character who fails an attempt to move faster than slow speed may make the check as many times as wished until successful.

When the golem arrives at this location, it continues pursuing the characters but suffers 1d10 points of damage from stumbling through the rubble strewn across the canyon floor.

8: A Hail of Arrows

As a characters come within 10' of this location, they may attempt a Wisdom [Perception] [DC 15] check. Any character who succeeds on the check notices that there are several pressure plates hidden on the canyon floor for the next 10 feet. Any character who steps on a pressure plate sets off an arrow trap *(see below)*.

Once a pressure plate has been detected, it can be avoided by stepping deliberately around it. The pressure plates can be disarmed by using spikes and passing a Dexterity check [DC 15]. Any character with thieves' tools makes the Dexterity check at advantage. If an attempt to disarm fails, the arrow trap triggers as normal *(see below)*.

Arrow Trap: Ranged attack, +6 bonus, 1d6 damage.

When the golem reaches this point of the canyon, it suffers 1d6x1d10 points of damage as it sets off several pressure plates on its slow march through the canyon.

9: Slippery When Wet

As the characters approach, read the following.

> You hear the roar of a waterfall long before you see it. You arrive upon a ledge where the waterfall has carved a large crevasse in the floor of the canyon. Several stone pillars, having survived centuries of water carving a path through the canyon, jut skyward. These wet, slippery pillars represent the best opportunity for you to cross the crevasse.

The most convenient way for the PCs to cross this ravine is either by using something like a Fly spell or by jumping from pillar to pillar. To jump to a pillar a character is required to make a Dexterity [Acrobatics] [DC 15] check. Any character who fails begins to fall, and unless stopped (such as by a rope tied around the waist) lands in the river below. There is no damage from the fall, but the character is required to pass a Strength [Athletics] [DC12] check to swim, or begins drowning. A drowning character suffers the effect of suffocation (PHB pg. 183) until making a successful swim check. A character who has fallen and is swimming may attempt to climb a stone pillar with a Strength [Athletics] [DC 10].

It is possible for a single character to make it across the ravine and then fasten a rope on the other side. This grants any characters using the rope a +5 on any skill checks required while crossing the ravine.

If the golem is still alive at this point, read the following regardless of how far the party is ahead of the creature..

> You hear the thundering steps of the golem that has chased you the length of the canyon. Its massive form emerges, moving in your direction. You can see that its journey through the canyon has taken a toll on the creature. It is no longer in the pristine condition it was when you first encountered it. With mindless determination, it continues to walk forward until it reaches the edge of the ravine. Without hesitation, it takes a final step, but its large foot finds no purchase. For several moments, the massive living statue teeters on the edge before finally falling. As it falls, it crushes the stone pillars you used only moments earlier to find passage across the ravine. You hear it crash when it collides with the river far below and know that you no longer need to fear the deadly blows and its endless stalking pursuit.

10: Lair of the Gorgon

You head away from the ravine that was the final demise of the golem. The walls of the canyon are scarred with large scratches as though some creature has smashed into them over and over again.

If a character approaches the lair of the gorgon, allow a Wisdom [Perception] check [DC 15]. If successful, several pieces of stone are observed scattered about the canyon floor. A Wisdom [Perception] check [DC 15] reveals that the bits of stone have tooth marks on them. If a character passes an Intelligence [Nature] check [DC 25], it can be surmised that these stones are the remnants of a gorgon's frequent meals.

The gorgon is the final encounter on this leg of the Marathon of Heroes (MM pg. 171). The gorgon immediately attacks any character it detects and fights to the death. If the gorgon is defeated, searching around the area of its lair reveals the following treasure.

105 SP
58 GP
2 small onyx gems worth 50 GP each
2 Potions of Healing
1 Ring of Fire Resistance +1
1 Short Sword +2/+4 vs. Dragons
1 Scroll of Greater Restoration

Once the characters are done searching the lair of the gorgon, they need to travel approximately 100 yards to reach the return stone. Touching the stone brings the party back to the beginning of the Marathon of Heroes.

A Trip to Hell

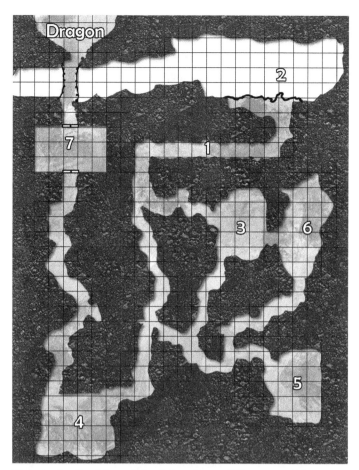

This is the final leg of the Marathon of Heroes and is literally a trip through hell. The party travels through lava tubes to face off against threats of literal hell. If the characters are not at least level 6 by this time, the GM may want to give the characters a level of experience and allow a long rest.

Regarding Gennifor and Geophry

Gennifor and Geophry are a pair of succubi (MM pg. 285) who have been imprisoned by the patron they served in hell. They must retrieve an item in the dragon's hoard called the Infernal Gem to be allowed to return to their home. The succubi and their minions attempted to battle the dragon when they were first banished to this location, but were soundly defeated. The pair and their minions have waited in hopes that someone or something might come along that improves their chances of defeating the dragon.

This portion of the module offers a lot of opportunity for roleplay. The GM should take some time to become familiar with the NPCs that are presented here as well as their motivations and desires.

You arrive back at the start of the marathon. This time things are different. Instead of five stones, there is only a single stone marked with the dragon sigil. The sigil radiates a strange glow and lunacy hangs in the air.

If Detect Magic is used, the stone radiates teleportation magic. If Detect Evil is used, the stone radiates an aura of evil. Anyone who touches the stone instantly teleports the entire party to Area 1 on the map.

Area Features

Throughout the maze of lava tunnels there are features that remain consistent unless otherwise noted.

All passages are 10' high and 10' wide and glow with heat that provides low visibility.

The heat within the tunnels is stifling but only harmful to those who have a weakness to heat. Any character with a weakness to heat must make a Constitution saving throw [DC 15] once per hour of game time or be exhausted until leaving the lava tunnels.

1. Welcome to Hell

You reach out and touch the stone with the dragon sigil. Instantly you find yourself standing in a winding tunnel. A glow radiates from the tunnel, allowing you to see normally. The heat that creates the glow makes the tunnel uncomfortably warm. The tunnel seems to go on for about 40' in each direction before it bends and you can no longer see what lies ahead.

Any character who succeeds on a Perception check [DC 10] hears the magma mephits in Area 2 at play. There is nothing else of interest in this location.

2. Lake of Lava

As you walk along the lava tube, the passage suddenly widens. A cavern opens, revealing a lake of lava. The floor of the cavern extends beyond the entrance 30' before its edge meets with the slowly flowing magma. The heat of the molten rock steals your breath away. Several dark red, winged creatures are flying over the lava, occasionally dipping into the molten rock to fly out moments later.

This cavern is home to 6 magma mephits (MM pg. 216). While they are evil in alignment, they do not attack any character unless harmed or threatened in some way. The mephits have been here a long time and have explored the lave tubes extensively. Any character who speaks Terran or Ignis can communicate with the mephits.

If a character speaks with the mephits, a Charisma [Persuasion] check will yield the following results.

DC 10 – They know there is a dragon just past the lake of magma but stay well away of him.

DC 15 – They have seen two humans wandering the passages of lava tubes. If asked to describe the humans, the mephits respond that all humans look alike.

DC 20 – The mephits know there are many devils who lair in the caverns found in other parts of the lava tubes.

DC 25 – The mephits know about the stone bridge that crosses the lava lake and can tell people where it is.

The heat of the lava lake is oppressive and requires a CON [Endurance] DC 15 roll to avoid heat exhaustion.

3. Bearded Devil Lair

Two bearded devils make their lair here. The bearded devils often spend their time tormenting the lemures in Area 6. Roll a d100 and consult the following table when the PCs approach.

Roll	Result
01 – 33	Both devils are in their lair.
34 – 66	Only one devil is in the lair; the other is in Area 6.
67 – 100	Both devils are in Area 6 tormenting the lemures.

If both bearded devils are present, they attack the moment they detect the party. If only one devil is present, it rushes to Area 6 to alert its partner. The two devils then attempt to ambush the party when it enters area 6. There is no treasure to be found here.

4. Barbed Devil Guard

Grichacht is a barbed devil (MM pg. 70) who has been summoned here as a guard by Gennifor and Geophry. He has no love for the two succubi and resents being forced to guard the tunnel that leads to their posh living quarters. For this reason, he is far more interested in making a deal with the PCs than he is in fighting them.

Grichacht does his best to get the PCs to agree to kill the succubi if they interact with him. He sees this as his only way out of imprisonment. He does not have anything to offer the PCs but is willing to aid them in their fight against the dragon if they agree to kill his succubi summoners. If the barbed devil feels he is losing negotiations or becomes frustrated, he attacks the party.

Should a fight go bad for Grichacht, he runs toward Area 7 to beg the pair of succubi for help.

5. Otyugh Pit

No one really knows how the otyugh [MM pg. 248] in this pit came to be here. The devils have given thought to killing the thing, but it does prove useful when they slay interlopers and don't want corpses stinking up the area.

6. Lemure Pool

Gennifor and Geophry were given several lesser devils to command when they were banished to the lava tubes. Several lemures were among these lesser devils. When the succubi do not have a need for the lemures, they are left in this area under the watch of the bearded devils in Area 3. If anyone but one of the other devils enters this area, the lemures mindlessly attack.

7. Gennifor and Geophry

The doors to this location are locked but may be opened with thieves' tools on a successful Dexterity check [DC 17].

Once the party gains access to the room, read the following.

As you open the doors an opulently decorated chamber is revealed. Fine tapestries adorn the walls, exquisite carpets lie on the floor, and in the middle of the room stands a table overflowing with a delicious looking banquet. Two extremely attractive humans dine at the table. One of them is a woman with long flowing red hair; the other is a man whose face is an ideal of masculine beauty.

The man smiles warmly as he stands, "Welcome brave adventurers. Please sit and enjoy a meal while my sister and I tell you of our plight."

The two humans are the succubi (MM pg. 84) Gennifor and Geophry disguising themselves. If the PCs choose to speak with them, the succubi attempt to persuade them to help in killing Vatrastrom. The pair knows that they need the dragon dead to retrieve the Infernal Gem and have been waiting decades for a group strong enough to help.

The succubi only care about retrieving the gem. They have grown very tired of languishing in their prison and want nothing more than to return to their home plane. If the party is willing to make a deal, the succubi offer the party five Potions of Resist Fire and everything in the Vatrastrom's hoard but the gem. Should the characters ask why the gem is so important, the succubi only tell them that they have no idea, only that they need to retrieve it before they are allowed to return to their realm.

The truth is that the Infernal Gem is of very little value.

The retrieval of the gem is an arbitrary task to delay and confound the succubi pair in the Lands of Lunacy.

If the PCs appear hostile or unwilling to help, both succubi attempt to charm one or more characters. If they are unable to charm a character or the characters attack, they attempt to kill the PCs.

The decorations and the food are all an illusion cast by the succubi. While the decorations may be fake, there is real treasure contained in a small wooden box near the back of the chamber.

Treasure:

345 CP
134 SP
105 GP
Five Potions of Resist Fire

9. Vatrastrom's Lair

A natural stone bridge spanning a 30' wide flow of lava lies 20' ahead of you. Beyond the bridge, a massive cavern stretches hundreds of feet overhead.

This cavern is 100' in diameter and 300' tall. Vatrastrom is a young red dragon (MM pg. 98) and has collected his hoard against the far wall. He spends his time here basking on the pile of treasure when he is not ravaging the countryside. Allow the dragon a passive Perception check when the PCs begin moving across the bridge. If Vatrastrom detects the party, he takes to the air, attacking as many party members as he can with his breath weapon.

If Gennifor and Geophry are with the party, they advise that stealth would be a good option. When the fight with Vatrastrom begins, they will do their best to avoid direct combat. If it looks like the party is going to lose the fight, they attempt to steal the gem they seek while the PCs distract the dragon.

Gennifor and Geophry keep their word and only take the Infernal Gem if the party defeats Vatrastrom. If it looks like the party intends to take the gem or attack the pair, one distracts the party while the other tries to reach the gem. Once one of the succubi retrieves the gem, both teleport to their home plane.

The PCs find a large crack in the north wall if they explore the cavern. This crack is where Vatrastrom entered and exited. Any character who uses this exit finds a 20' wide ledge with a teleportation stone. Anyone who touches the teleportation stone instantly teleports the party back to the beach where the Marathon of Heroes began.

Players are likely to be excited about the dragon hoard. Moving such a large amount of treasure (even with a bag of holding) may prove to be a difficult task.

Treasure:

10,923 CP
5,871 SP
2,300 GP
110 PP

8 gems worth 10 GP each (one of which is the Infernal Gem)
Wand of Magic Detection
Scroll of Speak with Dead
Potion of Growth

The Journey Home

You touch the stone outside the dragon's lair and find yourself standing on the beach where you first met Gundastav. When the murine notices you, he jumps from the log where he was perched and rushes to you. "Did you do it?" he asks, "Did you kill the dragon?"

Gundastav is elated when he hears the dragon is dead. He congratulates the heroes on a job well done and thanks them for ending the life of the tyrant his people have suffered under. After he congratulates everyone, Gundastav looks shamefully at the ground and says the following.

"The murine will always be thankful for what you have done, but I am afraid I must ask you for your help again. We have had our homes and fields destroyed by the dragon. I know it is shameful, but I must ask if you would be willing to part with some of your hard-earned treasure so that we may begin rebuilding our lives."

If the party agrees to give Gundastav some of its treasure, he is overjoyed and offers to host a ceremony of gratitude in honor of the party that evening. He also offers the aid of his people in retrieving any of the dragon's treasure that was left behind by the group.

If the heroes deny Gundastav's request, he accepts their decision sadly and departs. If the heroes left any treasure in the cavern, the murine gathers his people and tries to retrieve it before the party returns to the lair. They know the island very well and can move far faster than the party. It is up the GM if the murine are successful in this endeavor.

Once the party is ready to head home, it is time to return to the Sylph. When they arrive, read the following.

As you approach the boat, the first mate, James Millerson, comes running toward you. He arrives breathing heavily, a panicked look on his face.

"We have to move fast, the cephalugia attacked and killed everyone but me. I don't know how long we have. Hurry!"

James is lying. He is the one who killed the remaining crew and plans to do the same to the PCs once they are out to sea. The first night the party is at sea, James attempts to assassinate the characters. He waits until everyone is asleep. If the party posts a guard, he tries to silently kill whichever character is on guard with his assassination and poison talents. If the characters survive the assassination attempt, they arrive at harbor the next afternoon.

Lord Fez has been watching for the ship since the party left on the journey. When the heroes arrive at harbor, he is eager to greet them, insisting they show him the head of the dragon at once. Lord Fez is quite happy with the party and hosts them at his hold, throwing a lavish feast in their honor.

Appendix

Monsters and NPCs

Cephalugia

Medium aquatic creature, lawful evil

Cephalugia are braver in numbers, but individuals fight ferociously when cornered. They employ an ink defense to attempt escape when seriously injured or threatened.

Their favorite tactic is to use the grip strength of their tentacles to drag victims above or below the waterline until they suffocate. They then retrieve prey to consume at their leisure and collect trophies.

STR	DEX	CON	INT	WIS	CHR
16(+3)	9(-1)	14(+2)	8(-1)	9(-1)	12(+1)

AC 13, **HP** 18 (2d10 + 6), **Speed** 40 ft., swim 120 ft.

Size Adults 7–8' long
Skills Control/command lesser aquatic creatures
Damage Immunities most nematocyst stings (jellyfish & similar).
Condition immunity prone
Senses darkvision 30 ft., passive Perception 10
Languages Aquan
Challenge 1/2 (1100 XP)

Actions

Grapple. Cephalugia may attack a victim (ignoring armor protection) with the intent of grappling. Once grappled, they attempt to drag victims below the water until suffocation occurs. Once grappled with a single tentacle, the cephalugia has advantage on other tentacle attacks when attempting to further restrain victims.

Weapon. Melee weapon (usually spear or trident): +4 to hit, reach 5ft., one target. *Hit:* 7 (1d8 + 3) piercing damage.

Ink. (Recharge 2 hours) Cephalugia eject ink into the water when threatened or to confuse or surprise victims.

Bite. Melee: +4 to hit, reach 5ft., one target. *Hit:* 5 (1d6 + 3).

Giant Eel (electric)

Huge beast, unaligned

STR	DEX	CON	INT	WIS	CHR
19(+4)	14(+2)	12(+1)	1(-5)	10(0)	3(-4)

AC 12, **HP** 60 (8d12 + 8), **Speed** swim 60 ft.

Size Adults 10–16' long
Skills Perception +2
Senses blindsight 10', passive Perception 12
Challenge 2 (450 XP)

Actions

Bite. *Melee Weapon Attack:* +6 to hit, reach 10 ft., one creature. *Hit:* 11 (2d6 + 4) piercing damage.

Shock. (Recharge 5–6) *Area attack:* +6 to hit, reach 15'x15'x15' cube. *Hit:* 10 (2d6 + 4) electrical damage. Con save [DC 12] or stunned for 1d4 rounds.

Giant Stone Tortoise

Large beast, unaligned

Giant stone tortoises are large animals that have evolved to consume stone. As they eat stone, their digestive systems break down the minerals which are then used to strengthen the tortoises' shells. This process gives their shells a rough and rocky quality that deflects damage incredibly well.

STR	DEX	CON	INT	WIS	CHR
16(+3)	7(-2)	16(+3)	5(-3)	9(-1)	10(0)

AC 20, **HP** 35 (5d10 + 15), **Speed** 15 ft.

Size Adult 8' in diameter 6' high
Damage Immunities half damage from slashing and piercing weapons
Senses tremor sense (detects creatures walking on the ground within a 60' radius on successful Perception check), passive Perception 9
Languages None
Challenge 5 (1,800 XP)

Actions

Hide. When a giant stone tortoise is reduced to half HP or less, it hides inside its shell for 1d4 rounds. When inside its shell, the tortoise's metabolism speeds up and repairs damage done to its shell at a rate of 5 HP per round. It may only do this once per combat.

Stomp. (Recharge 5–6) The tortoise lifts a leg and stomps the ground, causing the earth to tremble. Any character within 10' of the tortoise must make a Dexterity save [DC 12] or fall prone.

Bite. Melee +6, reach 10', one target. *Hit:* 7 (1d8+3) piercing damage.

Giant Trap Door Spider
Large beast, unaligned

STR	DEX	CON	INT	WIS	CHR
14(+2)	16(+3)	12(+1)	2(-4)	11(0)	4(-3)

AC 14 (Natural armor), **HP** 26 (4d10 + 4), **Speed** 30 ft., climb 60' ft.

Skills Stealth +7
Senses: blindsight 10', darkvision 60', tremor sense 60'
Languages None
Challenge 2 (450 XP)

Spider Climb. Giant trap door spiders can climb any surface without penalty to speed or need to make climb checks.

Actions

Bite. *Melee weapon attack:* +5 to hit, reach 5ft., one creature. *Hit:* 1d8+3 piercing damage and target must make a Constitution save [DC 12] or take an additional 2d6 points of damage and become paralyzed. Victim may attempt a save each round. Success indicates the victim is no longer paralyzed.

Web. (Recharge 5–6) *Ranged attack:* +5. *Hit:* 1d6 damage and character is entangled. Character can break the webbing with a Strength check [DC 12]. The webbing can be damaged: AC 10; HP 5; vulnerability to fire damage, immune to bludgeoning, poison, and psychic damage.

Grush the Wolf Lord
Large humanoid (ogre, shapechanger), chaotic evil

STR	DEX	CON	INT	WIS	CHR
14(+2)	8(-1)	16(+3)	9(-1)	11(0)	12(+1)

AC 11 in ogre form (hide armor), 12 in wolf form (natural armor), **HP** 72 (9d10 + 27), **Speed** 30 ft. (40 ft. in wolf form)

Skills Perception +2, Stealth +1
Damage Immunities bludgeoning, slashing, and piercing damage from non-magical weapons that are not silvered
Senses darkvision 60', passive Perception 12
Languages Common, Giant
CR 5 (1,800 XP)

Shapechanger. Grush can change between ogre, wolf, and hybrid form at will. The change takes one round. Any equipment Grush is wearing does not change with him. Only armor class changes when Grush shapechanges into wolf or hybrid form.

Keen Hearing and Smell. Grush gains advantage on Wisdom checks that rely on hearing or smell.

Actions

Multi-attack (ogre or hybrid form only). Grush attacks with both a bite and weapon attack.

Bite (hybrid or wolf form only). *Melee Weapon Attack:* +4 to hit, 5' reach. *Hit:* 8 (1d8 + 4) piercing damage. If target is humanoid, it must make a Constitution saving throw [DC 12] or contract werewolf lycanthropy.

Great club (ogre or hybrid form only). *Melee Weapon Attack:* +6 to hit, reach 5 ft., one target. *Hit:* 13 (2d8 + 4) bludgeoning damage.

Claws (hybrid form only). *Melee Weapon Attack:* +4 to hit, 5 ft. reach. *Hit:* 10 (2d6 + 4) slashing damage.

Murine

Small Humanoid

Murine are small rodent-related humanoids. They live in tight social groups and are experts at hiding. Murine tend to avoid conflict when possible.

STR	DEX	CON	INT	WIS	CHR
8(-1)	16(+3)	12(+1)	10(0)	10(0)	12(+1)

AC 14 (natural armor), **HP** 5 (1d8+1), **Speed** 25 ft.

Size small
Skills Stealth +4, Perception +3,
Senses acute hearing, acute smell, darkvision 40 ft.
Challenge 1/4

Actions

Claw, *Melee attack* +2 to hit, reach 5 ft., one target. *Hit:* 2 (1d6-1).
Bite. Melee attack +2 to hit, reach 5', one target, *Hit:* 3 (1d8-1)
Melee Attack. By weapon type.
Ranged Attack. By weapon type.

Vatrastrom the Red Menace

Large Dragon

Vatrastrom is a young red dragon who is small and a relatively weak example of his kind. While Vatrastrom may be smaller and weaker than other red dragons his age, he is still a very fearsome foe. Vatrastrom is quite arrogant after having spent so many years without challenge to his rule and will not unload his breath weapon until the battle starts to turn against him.

STR	DEX	CON	INT	WIS	CHR
20(+5)	10(0)	18(+4)	14(+2)	11(0)	19(+4)

AC 18 (natural armor), **HP** 178 (17d10+85), **Speed** 40ft. **climb** 40ft., **fly** 80ft.
Size small, **Saving Throws** Dex +4, Con +7, Wis +4, Cha +8

Skills Perception +8, Stealth +4
Senses Blindsight 30ft., darkvision 120ft., passive Perception 18
Challenge 10 (5,900 XP)

Actions

Multiattack. The dragon makes three attacks: one with its bite and two with claws.

Bite. Melee Weapon Attack. +8 to hit, reach 10ft., one target. *Hit:* 17 (2d8 + 5) piercing damage.

Claw. Melee Weapon Attack: +8 to hit, reach 5 ft., one target, *Hit:* l3 (2d4 + 5) slashing damage.

Fire Breath. (Recharge 5-6). The dragon exhales fire in a 30-foot cone. Each creature in that area must make a [DC 17] Dexterity saving throw, taking 30 (l0d6) fire damage on a failed save, or half as much on a successful one.

The Warrior
Medium Magical Construct

Where the Warrior came from or who created it is unknown. Murine myth suggests that the warrior was originally a gift from their gods tasked with protecting their race. If this is true, the warrior has forgotten that oath and now is contained inside a circle of salt where it waits to challenge all who are willing to risk death.

STR	DEX	CON	INT	WIS	CHR
18(+4)	10(0)	14(+2)	10(0)	10(0)	10(0)

AC 18 (Full Plate Mail), **HP** 60 (10d10+10), **Speed** 30

Size Medium
Skills nil
Senses Perception +2, darkvision 50 ft.
Challenge 3

Actions

Sword, Melee Weapon Attack +8 to hit, reach 5 ft., *Hit:* 8 (1d8+4)

Magic Items

Armor of the Battlefield

Armor (full plate), unique (requires attunement)

Armor of the Battlefield is equivalent to +2 Full Plate Armor of Fire Resistance but is cursed.

Curse: When a character attunes to this item during a short rest, the curse activates. This curse binds the armor to the character's body and cannot be removed. The armor does not allow the face guard to be moved, and thus the character cannot eat. To gain sustenance the character must pour the blood of fallen enemies over the armor. If the character goes more than 24 hours without pouring blood over the armor, starvation begins. If the armor is removed, the curse is still active and can affect the same character again.

Leather Armor of Nimbleness

Armor (leather), very rare (requires attunement)

Leather Armor of Nimbleness is +1 leather armor that also grants the wearer +1 to all Dexterity saves and Dexterity related skills.

Robes of the Dragon Mage

Wondrous Item (robes), very rare (requires attunement: Wizard)

The Robes of the Dragon Mage were created long ago to aid wizards in combating dragons. Each set of robes gives resistance to a specific dragon's breath weapon. Robes of the Red Dragon Mage give resistance against a red dragon's breath weapon, Robes of the Green Dragon Mage give resistance against a green dragon's breath weapon, etc.

This resistance reduces any damage caused by a dragon's breath weapon by half. If a saving throw would have reduced the damage by half, then the robes reduce the damage to 0.

Character Name

◯ Inspiration

◯ Proficiency Bonus

Strength

◯

Dexterity

◯

Constitution

◯

Intelligence

◯

Wisdom

◯

Charisma

◯

Class & Level   Background   Player Name

Race   Alignment   Experience Points

Armor Class	Initiative	Speed	Hit Dice	Death Saves
				Success ◯◯◯
				Fail ◯◯◯

○ _____ Strength
○ _____ Dexterity
○ _____ Constitution
○ _____ Intelligence
○ _____ Wisdom
○ _____ Charisma

Saving Throws

○ _____ Acrobatics(Dex)
○ _____ Animal
○ _____ Handling(Wis)
○ _____ Arcana(Int)
○ _____ Athletics(Str)
○ _____ Deception(Cha)
○ _____ History(Int)
○ _____ Insight(Wis)
○ _____ Intimidation(Cha)
○ _____ Investigation(Int)
○ _____ Medicine(Wis)
○ _____ Nature(Int)
○ _____ Perception(Wis)
○ _____ Performance(Cha)
○ _____ Persuasion(Cha)
○ _____ Religion(Int)
○ _____ Sleight of Hand(Dex)
○ _____ Stealth(Dex)
_____ Survival(Wis)

Skills

◯ Passive Perception

Proficiencies & Languages

Hit Point Maximum ◯

Current Hit Points

Temporary Hit Points

Name   Bonus   Damage/Type

_____
_____
_____
_____
_____
_____
_____

Attacks & Spellcasting

Sanity - Wis + 3/ Level base

CP
SP
EP
GP
PP

Equipment

Personality Traits

Ideals

Bonds

Flaws

Features/Traits

Murine as Players

The murine are intelligent anthropomorphic natives of the Lands of Lunacy and, as their name suggests, are a rodent race. They retain many of their rodent qualities: fur, facial features, and body type. Not all murine are physically the same, some resembling rats, mice, or even guinea pigs. All are very social creatures whatever their appearance.

The murine may not be imposing individually, but when acting as a communal mind, their ferocity can bewilder even the most bloodthirsty savage.

They have a deep love and appreciation for music and the arts. Music could be considered a weakness of the murine, if they have one other than being remarkably good with intentions. Such is their appreciation for music that the murine are particularly susceptible to bardic magic.

All bardic effects created by music, gain an additional +1 bonus if the listener happens to be murine.

The murine love creature comforts and community. They are ambitious and have a strong work ethic with a desire to

see what lies ahead of the next vista. The average murine is approximately 3 feet tall and favors light weapons such as daggers, rapiers, small bows, and darts.

The murine love fine fabrics and tailored clothing but detest shoes. Shoes inhibit their claws and ability to climb or dig and are painfully uncomfortable and clumsy. Clothes are not necessary in murine society, only appreciated for the aesthetic.

There exists numerous sub-races of murine that vary in appearance and genetics. Most of the sub-races are akin to Prime Material Plane native cavies (guinea pigs), mice, rats, and similar rodents.

There remains in murine folklore, the tale of a long-lost relative of giant proportions that resembled the capybara. The tales of these legendary murine giants paint them as 7-foot-tall warriors, figuring largely in fanciful tales often told to younglings around a campfire. Even though a capybara-type would not be a murine proper, the murine solidly claim these jungle heroes of adventure as their own relatives.

Sub-races intermingle freely, marry, and form families. However, nature and biology rarely allow for sub-races to successfully interbreed. The children are always sterile if mixed sub-races bear young.

Murine society is quite open and centered around individual freedoms and happiness while serving and connecting to the community. Families and households may consist of any gender or sub-race or number of combinations. The murine who seek a life of adventure seek groups that they feel will help them survive and who share a sense of communal support. Once this relationship is established, the adventuring murine will do everything they can to make themselves valuable members of the adventuring party.

A portion of every murine's day is spent serving the community in some way. These services typically include preparing food for others, milling lumber or wheat, building homes, or doing farm chores. Each murine does this gladly, and such work is frequently followed with grooming their neighbors and other community members who find themselves involved. The murine take great pleasure in grooming one another frequently and thoroughly. It solidifies their bonds and connections within their community and minimizes mites, fleas, and other problematic insects.

Murine are susceptible to depression if they go more than three days without participating in their own community or one they have adopted. Community participation does not necessarily require other murine to find happiness. Humans or other races, however, frequently find thorough communal grooming to be uncomfortable or outright unacceptable.

Murine society, while quite communal in nature, frequently defers to an agreed-upon leader who is elevated to king, queen, lord, lady, or whatever title the community deems appropriate. The leader is not exempted from community service and bears responsibility of general leadership. If a leader's rule becomes disagreeable to the community, the leader is removed from the position and replaced quickly with little debate.

The murine have little use for coin or currency within their communities. They do, however, appreciate the uses of currency outside their society. Some murine, especially those related to pack rats, collect coins and valuables to trade for fine fabrics and silks. The murine are also likely to collect precious metals simply for their aesthetic decorative appeal.

Murine can survive comfortably in sewers and tunnels, burrows, or anywhere they find themselves. They prefer warmm dry homes and hearth fires wherever they can find them. They are skilled craftsmen when they choose a profession. Murine who choose a craft pursue it with great single-minded passion.

The murine regularly train and groom large creatures from birth as protection for their communities. Many murine villages have bears, large cats, dire wolves, or other creatures native to the Lands of Lunacy incorporated into their guard patrols. There are only 1d4 of such creatures per average community, but they are considered exceptional animals, with maximum hit points and are expertly trained and cared for by the entire community.

The murine retain many rodent abilities: darkvision, keen senses of smell and hearing, climbing ability, and stealth. This makes them excellent thieves and scouts. The murine are not inclined toward theft among their own kind–such activity disrupts the bonds of community. Thieving outside the murine community is viewed as something more akin to "cleaning up" or "reducing waste". Packrat related murine favor the secret exchange of goods over theft.

Life Span

Murine reach adulthood at 5 years of age and rarely live beyond 40. They celebrate frequently and live passionately, but are almost always cautious to not celebrate to excess or completely be left flat-footed.

Murine Names

The Murine language consists of squeaks, chatter, and other sounds that can be difficult for other races to mimic. For this reason, most murine adopt a "traveling" or "trading" name to use amongst non-murine. Murine tend to have more contact with humanity than other races native to the Lands of Lunacy, thus, their traveling names are often names humans would use or find appealing.

Among themselves, murine frequently "Find their name" during their coming of age ceremony when they reach adulthood at 5 years old. Younglings less than 5 frequently experiment with giving themselves names to try out. They also respond to "Youngling" as they are commonly addressed by adults.

Native names (non-traveling names) frequently reflect the murine's passion, craft, or activities:

Ring Trader, Gleam Chaser, Grey Archer, Acorn Keep, Tree Hide, etc.

The names properly spoken are mostly a combination of chitters and squeaks.

Murine in frequent contact with other societies may also adapt a name from that society when they come of age, and members of the community do the best they can to accommodate.

Murine Traits

Ability Score Increase. Murine gain a +2 to their dexterity.

GM option. Murine are typically not strong creatures. A penalty of -1 STR may be optionally imposed on murine PCs at character creation.

Age. Murine have short life spans and seldom live past the age of 40. Murine reach adulthood within five years

Alignment. Because of their communal nature, the murine respect law and order, but only as it applies to their own society. The Murine are almost never evil, such beings would be cast out of the community, which is worse than death for the interdependent creatures.

Size. Murine average 3' in height and are considered small.

Speed. Murine may be small but they have adapted to move quickly. A murine has a walking speed of 30', and when naked can gallop on all fours.

Darkvision. Murine are accustomed to living underground and operating at night. They have developed darkvision up to 40 feet.

Keen Senses: A murine has incredibly keen senses. They gain proficiency in perception and always roll with advantage.

Diurnal: Murine need a limited amount of sleep. They are extremely proficient "nappers". A murine only needs to sleep for four hours (once every twelve hours) to gain the benefits of a long rest. A murine that goes longer than 12 hours without sleeping must sleep for eight hours to gain the benefits of a long rest.

Nervous Nature: Murine are always aware of their surroundings. For this reason, they often find the best place to hide and gain a +2 racial bonus on all stealth related checks.

Climbers: Murine without shoes gain +1 to all climbing rolls and are proficient in the Athletics skill.

Languages: Murine are fascinated by humans and elves, and adore many of the halfling attitudes toward life. They can speak, read, and write Murine and speak Common. Although an oral history is more common among Murine than a written one.

Lunacy Resilience: Murine are native to the Lands of Lunacy and therefore typically do not suffer the effects of the realm. They may suffer mental and physical effects from extended exposure to the Prime Material Plane.

CPSIA information can be obtained
at www.ICGtesting.com
Printed in the USA
LVHW101933101218
599938LV00034B/1289/P